Meow T

Embracing the Wise Ways of the Taoist Kitty Lifestyle

By Ellen Johnson

MEOW TE CHING : Embracing the Wise Ways of the Taoist Kitty Lifestyle

Copyright ©2023 by Ellen Johnson

All rights reserved. No part of this book may be reproduced or used in any form without written permission from the publisher.

ISBN-13: 979-8-9886886-1-7 (Paperback)
ISBN-13: 979-8-9886886-0-0 (Hardback)
ISBN-13: 979-8-9886886-2-4 (Coloring Book)

Library of Congress Control Number: 2023912919

Original graphics By: www.etsy.com/shop/yupiyeigraphics

First printing, 2023

Publisher: Ellen Johnson, P.O. Box 1871, Melbourne, FL 32902
Email: Ellen@MeowTeChing.com

MeowTeChing.com

To my boys, who unknowingly embody the innate qualities of the Tao, have taught me invaluable lessons. I love you both so much.

Joshua Otis, you possess a genuine and unassuming nature that is non-judgmental and open, evident to everyone you encounter.

Samuel Chase, a man of few words, your simplicity and silence speak volumes, revealing wisdom beyond your years.

For countless years, cats have shown us how to live simply and truthfully. They naturally embody this way of life, unaware of any other. In this tale, I have blended the wisdom of Lao Tzu's Tao Te Ching with the behaviors, attitudes, and thoughts of my beloved cat, Zorro. My aim is to bring both amusement and a childlike understanding of the Tao in simpler terms. This book is meant for children, cats, and adults alike.

Ellen & Zorro

The Book Of Virtue

The Tao is a secret guide for all kitties on how to live a life of peace and happiness. By becoming better kitties, we help contribute to a more peaceful kitty world.

Non-Doing

The Tao is an invitation to a special, quiet place within ourselves where we can find stillness and happiness without having to do anything. No one can sell it to us (as it can't be purchased), nor can anyone take it away.

Nature

I love to smell the beautiful flowers and feel the cool breeze on my fur. This peaceful feeling, the Tao says, is a way of being in harmony with the earth. Being out in nature is like a kitty playground, there is so much beauty all around, I just need to take the time to look for it.

Harmony & Wisdom

The Tao shows us that it's important to live in harmony with others and to respect the wisdom of the wise cats that came before us.

Compassion

When I choose to be nice to others, the Tao says that I make the world a more peaceful place.

Inner Peace

In the sunshine, rain, or in life's highs or lows, we kitties are naturally born with a great sense of balance (we always land on our feet). The Tao reminds us to avoid extremes and find the middle path that brings us stability and peace.

Non-Attachment

As an independent kitty, the Tao teaches me to not get attached to too many things. I try to enjoy each moment of every day and accept things as they are. I find that life is more peaceful this way.

Inner Strength

The Tao shows me that as I develop a strong character and a calm mind, I will be able to face all of life's challenges. Life with the Tao makes every day go more smoothly.

Change

Sometimes I don't feel so happy when things change or don't go the way I want them to. The Tao tells me to find strength in being flexible. It says the world is full of change and never stays the same but I can always be happy in discovering new things.

Humility

The Tao shows me how to be humble. I don't need to show off or be super loud. I am happy with everything I already have and don't need anything else to bring me happiness.

Mystery

Being a curious kitty, I feel right at home with the Tao because I look at the world with awe and wonder. Each day brings a new adventure. I know that not everything in the world can be fully understood but because of the Tao, I am ok with it.

Silence

Although I like to be around my other kitty friends, I also find that I need some quiet time by myself. The Tao teaches that there is hidden wisdom in silence if I take the time to listen for it.

Peacefulness

Living by the Tao is like taking a peaceful cat nap. My kitty mind becomes quiet, and I feel calm on the inside. I make sure to take a cat nap every day because I love feeling this way.

Simplicity

Having less is easier for me than having too much. Having less means I have fewer troubles in my life. By not wanting too much and being happy with the simple pleasures around me, I can live a happy and peaceful life.

Patience

Living by the Tao means being patient with others as well as myself. I get along best with others when I don't force or rush them to do anything.

Printed in Great Britain
by Amazon